Navigating Sustainable Seas

OrangeBooks Publication

1st Floor, Rajhans Arcade, Mall Road, Kohka, Bhilai, Chhattisgarh 490020

Website: **www.orangebooks.in**

© Copyright, 2024, Author

All rights reserved. No part of this book may be reproduced, stored in a retrieval system, or transmitted, in any form by any means, electronic, mechanical, magnetic, optical, chemical, manual, photocopying, recording or otherwise, without the prior written consent of its writer.

First Edition, 2024

NAVIGATING SUSTAINABLE SEAS

A COMPREHENSIVE GUIDE TO CARBON MARKETS AND TRADING

DR. CHIRAG BHIMANI

OrangeBooks Publication
www.orangebooks.in

Table of Contents

Foreword xi

Preface xvii

Introduction xxi

Chapter - 1 1

Understanding The Need for Carbon Markets 3

1.1 Defining Climate Change and Its Implications 3

1.2 Introducing Carbon Markets as a Response to Climate Change 6

Chapter - 2 11

The Basics of Carbon Trading 13

2.1 Outlining The Fundamentals of Carbon Markets . 13

2.2 Explaining The Different Types of Carbon Credits 16

2.3 Detailing The Mechanisms of Emissions Trading Schemes (ETS) and Cap and Trade Systems 19

2.4 Analyzing The Key Players in The Carbon Trading Landscape 23

Chapter - 3 27

International Carbon Market Mechanisms 29

3.1 Exploring The Architecture of International Carbon Markets 29

3.2 Evaluating The Compliance and Voluntary Carbon Markets 31

3.3 Examining The United Nations Framework Convention on Climate Change (UNFCCC) Initiatives, Such as The Clean Development Mechanism (CDM) and the Paris Agreement 35

Chapter - 4 39

Carbon Market Instruments and Standards 41

4.1 Unveiling the Different Carbon Market Instruments and Their Peculiarities 41

4.2 Demonstrating the Significance of Carbon Pricing and Its Methodologies 44

4.3 Identifying Various Carbon Market Standards and Certifications 48

Chapter - 5 53

Carbon Market Participants and Trading Strategies 55

5.1 Profiling the Major Players in Carbon Markets, Including Governments, Project Developers, and Financial Institutions 55

5.2 Analyzing Successful Carbon Trading Strategies Adopted 59

5.3 Discussing Risk Management and Mitigation Techniques in Carbon Trading 64

Chapter - 6 71

Investment Opportunities in Carbon Markets 73

6.1 Highlighting the Potential Investment Avenues Within Carbon Markets 73

6.2 Evaluating the Financial Value of Carbon Credits and Their Market Trends 76

6.3 Unraveling the Challenges and Opportunities in Green Finance and Impact Investing 80

Chapter - 7 85

Carbon Market Regulations and Policies 87

7.1 Delving into the Regulatory Frameworks Governing Carbon Markets Worldwide 87

7.2 Examining the Role of National and Regional Policies in Promoting Carbon Trading 90

7.3 Assessing the Potential Impact of Future Regulations on Carbon Markets 94

Chapter - 8 99

Case Studies and Success Stories 101

8.1 Showcasing Real-World Case Studies of Successful Carbon Market Projects 101

8.2 Drawing Lessons from These Cases to Inspire and Encourage Future Market Participants 105

Chapter - 9 111

Carbon Market Outlook And Future Trends 113

9.1 Presenting an Overview of The Current State of Global Carbon Markets 113

9.2 Predicting Future Trends and Opportunities in The Sector 117

9.3 Forecasting the Potential Impact of Emerging Technologies on Carbon Markets 122

Way Forward 127

Notes 131

• ● •

Foreword

Humankind has faced many crises in the past, but few have been as daunting as climate change. Labelled a "super-wicked problem" due to its complexity, scale, time horizon, and the ubiquity of its causes and impacts, climate change evades coordinated management through traditional policy interventions. To be effective, any solution will ideally be scalable and able to range from the local to the global level, minimize the impact of information asymmetries by delegating decisions to the actors most familiar with opportunities and circumstances, offer flexibility to minimize compliance cost, and unlock private capital flows to meet the unprecedented levels of investment – estimated to exceed several trillion U.S. dollars every year for the coming decades – needed to decarbonize our economies and strengthen resilience against the unavoidable impacts of climate change.

Carbon markets offer such a policy solution. As a means of pricing carbon, they help correct one of the central market failures underlying climate change, the unpriced externality of greenhouse gas emissions. Faced by a carbon price signal, emitters are compelled to reflect the cost of carbon in their economic decisions. Because of the flexibility that emitters enjoy under this policy, they can choose to comply with climate targets through internal abatement or reliance on the market. Economic theory confirms that, in equilibrium, a carbon market achieves a Pareto-efficient outcome in which no emitter can reduce emissions at lower cost than anyone else, meaning that emission reductions are achieved at the lowest cost possible. Estimates suggest that global carbon trading could halve the cost of achieving the goals of the Paris Agreement.

And, importantly, carbon markets leverage finance to address climate change. Through the carbon price signal, they channel capital into emissions abatement activities and low-carbon innovation, helping close a substantial investment shortfall currently hampering progress on decarbonization. Such investment can also take shape of financial transfers from advanced economies to developing countries, thereby contributing to international climate finance and aiding low-carbon development in rapidly growing economies around the world. Finally, they can be designed to yield revenue – through auctioning of emissions allowances and deduction of proceeds – for public budgets, which are increasingly strained by rising debt and interest rates.

Globally, the steady – if occasionally turbulent – expansion of carbon markets, from various segments in the voluntary carbon market to subnational, national and regional compliance markets all the way to international frameworks such as Article 6 of the Paris Agreement or the Carbon Offsetting and Reduction Scheme for International Aviation (CORSIA), reflects the beneficial potential of this policy option. Already, carbon markets cover around 18% of global greenhouse gas emissions through a dozen national or supranational and over two dozen subnational emissions trading systems as well as mandatory or voluntary offset crediting schemes. Currently, these mechanisms raise over US$ 50 billion annually for public budgets.

As carbon markets continue this growth trajectory, with the development frontier shifting to emerging economies in Africa, Asia and Latin America, trading volumes – including international transfers – will only increase. Against that dynamic backdrop, "Navigating Sustainable Seas: A Comprehensive Guide to Carbon Markets and Trading" appears at the very best moment in time. A beacon of clarity and insight, it charts a path through the intricacies of carbon markets, offering a comprehensive roadmap for navigating the complexities of carbon trading and providing readers with valuable perspectives, strategies, and tools to engage in these innovative markets and catalyze meaningful change.

The title, "Navigating Sustainable Seas," encapsulates the essence of this guide, evoking a parallel between the challenges of traversing vast and unpredictable oceans and the intricacies of designing, implementing and subsequently operating within voluntary or compliance carbon markets. Just as seafarers have always relied on navigational tools, charts, and expertise to sail turbulent waters, policymakers, businesses, and stakeholders require informed guidance to harness the potential of carbon markets. Fortunately, this book offers a compass, illuminating pathways towards a more sustainable future by demystifying carbon markets, elucidating trading mechanisms, and highlighting best practices from around the globe.

The significance of this guide extends well beyond academic debate and theoretical scholarship. Carbon markets are increasingly a reality around the world that public and private decision makers and other stakeholders have to contend with, raising challenges as well as opportunities. By developing a nuanced understanding of carbon trading, readers will be empowered to engage proactively in shaping policy frameworks, driving innovation, and unlocking economic opportunities while mitigating environmental impacts. The diverse perspectives, case studies, and insights contained within these pages offer a holistic view of the carbon market landscape, transcending traditional disciplinary boundaries and fostering cooperation.

As we venture to address the complex and interconnected challenges of the 21st century, "Navigating Sustainable Seas" provides an indispensable resource for policymakers, business leaders, academics, and civil society stakeholders grappling with one of the most promising solutions. As a book, it transcends conventional narratives, inspiring readers to envision a future in which sustainability, innovation, and economic prosperity converge. I commend the author for his visionary approach, dedication, and commitment to advancing our collective understanding of the rapidly evolving carbon market, paving the way for a more resilient, equitable, and sustainable world.

May this guide serve as both a trusted companion and inspiration in your journey towards greater sustainability across all three dimensions of this term: social, economic, and environmental sustainability. I wish you, the reader, an exciting and enlightened journey through the turbulent seas of carbon trading, relying on this important reference work to ensure you reach your destination safely and expeditiously.

Prof. Dr. Michael Mehling

(Dr. Michael Mehling is Deputy Director of the MIT Center for Energy and Environmental Policy Research and a Professor at the University of Strathclyde Law School. He is also a non-executive director with Ecologic Institute in Berlin, a Manager of the Konrad-von-Moltke Fund in Berlin, and a founding board member of Ecologic Institute in Washington DC, the Blockchain & Climate Institute (BCI) in London, and the European Roundtable on Climate Change and Sustainable Transition (ERCST) in Brussels.)

• ● •

Preface

As we stand at the intersection of environmental stewardship, economic innovation, and policy evolution, the imperative to navigate the intricate waters of carbon markets and trading has never been more pressing. "Navigating Sustainable Seas: A Comprehensive Guide to Carbon Markets and Trading" emerges from a collective endeavor to illuminate the complexities, challenges, and opportunities inherent in this dynamic landscape. This book is born out of a shared commitment to fostering sustainability, promoting informed dialogue, and catalyzing actionable insights in an era defined by climate change, economic transformation, and global interdependence.

The genesis of this guide stems from recognizing a glaring gap in accessible, comprehensive resources that demystify carbon markets and trading for a diverse audience. While the discourse surrounding carbon markets often veers into specialized jargon, fragmented perspectives, and abstract concepts, this book endeavors to distill complex ideas into digestible insights, practical strategies, and real-world applications. Through a collaborative effort spanning experts, practitioners, and thought leaders, "Navigating Sustainable Seas" synthesizes diverse viewpoints, methodologies, and case studies to provide readers with a holistic, nuanced understanding of carbon markets and trading mechanisms.

The journey through these pages traverses a multifaceted landscape, encompassing regulatory frameworks, market dynamics, technological innovations, and stakeholder engagement strategies. Each chapter unfolds a distinct facet of the carbon ecosystem, weaving together theoretical foundations with empirical evidence, best practices with emerging trends, and global perspectives with localized insights. Whether you are a seasoned professional navigating the complexities of carbon trading or a newcomer seeking to grasp the fundamentals of this evolving landscape, this guide offers a comprehensive, accessible, and insightful roadmap to inform, inspire, and guide your journey.

At its core, "Navigating Sustainable Seas" is more than a book; it is a testament to collective collaboration, interdisciplinary synergy, and shared aspirations for a sustainable future. It embodies the spirit of inquiry, innovation, and inclusivity, inviting readers to engage critically, reflect deeply, and act decisively in shaping a world where economic prosperity aligns seamlessly with environmental integrity. As you embark on this exploration of carbon markets and trading, may you find inspiration, clarity, and purpose in navigating the sustainable seas that define our global journey towards a resilient, equitable, and sustainable future.

With gratitude for your curiosity, commitment, and contributions to this vital discourse, I invite you to embark on this transformative journey through the pages of "Navigating Sustainable Seas," forging pathways, fostering partnerships, and charting a course towards a brighter tomorrow for all.

Dr. Chirag Bhimani

Introduction

Welcome to "A Comprehensive Guide to Carbon Markets and Trading." In an era defined by environmental challenges and a collective call for sustainable practices, the concept of carbon markets has emerged as a pivotal force in the global fight against climate change. This guide is designed to serve as a compass, guiding readers through the intricate terrain of carbon markets and trading.

The Urgency of Climate Action:

As the impacts of climate change become increasingly evident, there is a growing sense of urgency to mitigate the effects of rising greenhouse gas emissions. Governments, businesses, and individuals are recognizing the need for decisive action to transition towards a low-carbon future. Carbon markets, with their ability to incentivize emission reductions and promote sustainable practices, have become a cornerstone in the endeavor to address climate change effectively.

Defining Carbon Markets:

Carbon markets, often referred to as emissions trading or cap-and-trade systems, represent a market-based approach to reducing greenhouse gas emissions. At their core, these markets create economic incentives for organizations to limit their carbon footprint by either reducing emissions directly or investing in projects that sequester or offset emissions elsewhere. This guide aims to unravel the complexities of carbon markets, providing a comprehensive understanding of their mechanisms, evolution, and impact on global sustainability efforts.

The Evolution of Carbon Markets:

The history of carbon markets traces back to the early 1990s, with the implementation of cap-and-trade systems in response to environmental challenges, particularly acid rain. Over the years, these markets have evolved, expanding in scope and scale to address the complex and interconnected challenges of climate change. From the Kyoto Protocol to the Paris Agreement, international efforts have shaped the trajectory of carbon markets, reflecting a shared commitment to a sustainable and resilient future.

The Structure of This Guide:

This guide is structured to provide a comprehensive overview of carbon markets, catering to a diverse audience ranging from policymakers and environmentalists to investors and business leaders. Each chapter delves into a specific aspect of carbon markets, from the fundamental principles and market mechanisms to emerging trends, technological innovations, and the forecasted future landscape.

The Intersection of Economics and Environment:

Carbon markets represent a unique intersection of economics and environmental conservation. The guide will explore how market-based mechanisms can drive positive environmental outcomes while fostering economic growth.

By understanding the intricate balance between financial incentives and ecological responsibility, readers will gain insights into how carbon markets can be leveraged as powerful tools for sustainable development.

A Call to Action:

As we embark on this exploration of carbon markets, it is essential to recognize that the challenges posed by climate change require collective and immediate action.

This guide encourages readers not only to comprehend the intricacies of carbon markets but also to consider their role in shaping the future. Whether you are a policymaker shaping regulations, a business leader navigating market dynamics, or an individual seeking sustainable choices, the knowledge within these pages is a resource to inform and inspire action.

Join us on this journey through the carbon market landscape. Together, let us navigate the complexities, embrace the opportunities, and contribute to a more sustainable and resilient future for our planet.

• ● •

Chapter - 1

Dr. Chirag Bhimani

Understanding The Need for Carbon Markets

1.1 Defining Climate Change and Its Implications

Introduction:

Climate change is a complex and pressing global issue that has garnered significant attention in recent years. It refers to long-term shifts in weather patterns and average temperatures on Earth, primarily caused by human activities. This chapter aims to provide a comprehensive understanding of climate change, its causes, and the implications it has on various aspects of our lives.

Defining Climate Change:

Climate change is the alteration of Earth's climate system, including its atmosphere, oceans, land surface, and ice sheets. It is primarily driven by the increase in greenhouse gas **(GHG)** emissions, such as carbon dioxide **(CO_2)** and methane **(CH_4)**, resulting from human activities like burning fossil fuels, deforestation, and industrial processes. These GHGs trap heat in the atmosphere, leading to a rise in global temperatures, commonly referred to as global warming.

Causes of Climate Change:

Human activities are the primary drivers of climate change. The burning of fossil fuels, such as coal, oil, and natural gas, for energy production and transportation releases large amounts of CO_2 into the atmosphere. Deforestation, which contributes to around 10% of global GHG emissions, reduces the Earth's capacity to absorb CO_2. Additionally, industrial processes, agriculture, and waste management also release significant amounts of GHGs.

Implications of Climate Change:

The implications of climate change are far-reaching and affect various aspects of our lives, including:

Environmental Implications:

Climate change leads to rising global temperatures, resulting in the melting of polar ice caps and glaciers and rising sea levels. This poses a significant threat to coastal communities, increasing the risk of flooding and erosion. Changes in precipitation patterns can also lead to more frequent and intense droughts, heatwaves, hurricanes, and other extreme weather events.

Ecological Implications:

Climate change disrupts ecosystems and threatens biodiversity. Many species struggle to adapt to rapidly changing conditions, leading to habitat loss, species extinction, and imbalances in ecosystems. This, in turn, affects food chains, pollination, and the overall health of ecosystems.

Economic Implications:

The economic implications of climate change are substantial. Extreme weather events can cause significant damage to infrastructure, agriculture, and property, resulting in financial losses. Additionally, industries reliant on natural resources, such as agriculture, fisheries, and tourism may face disruptions due to changing climate patterns.

Social Implications:

Climate change disproportionately affects vulnerable communities, exacerbating social inequalities. Impacts include increased food and water insecurity, displacement of populations due to rising sea levels or extreme weather events, and health risks associated with heat waves and the spread of diseases.

Conclusion:

Defining climate change and understanding its implications is crucial for developing effective strategies to mitigate its effects. Recognizing the causes and consequences of climate change allows us to take collective action to reduce GHG emissions, adapt to changing conditions, and work towards a sustainable future.

By addressing climate change, we can protect our environment, preserve biodiversity, and ensure a better quality of life for future generations.

1.2 Introducing Carbon Markets as a Response to Climate Change

Climate change is one of the most pressing global challenges of our time, with far-reaching implications for the environment, economy, and society. As the world grapples with the need to reduce greenhouse gas emissions, various strategies and mechanisms have been developed to mitigate the impacts of climate change. One such mechanism is the introduction of carbon markets, which aim to incentivize emission reductions and promote sustainable practices. This chapter provides an overview of carbon markets and their role in addressing climate change.

Understanding Carbon Markets:

Carbon markets, also known as emissions trading systems or cap-and-trade systems, are market-based approaches that put a price on carbon emissions. The basic principle behind carbon markets is to create a financial incentive for industries and organizations to reduce their greenhouse gas emissions. By assigning a monetary value to carbon emissions, carbon markets encourage the adoption of cleaner technologies and practices.

How Carbon Markets Work:

In a carbon market, a regulatory body sets a limit, or cap, on the total amount of greenhouse gas emissions allowed within a specific jurisdiction or sector. This cap is then divided into individual allowances, each representing a specific amount of emissions. These allowances can be bought, sold, or traded among participants in the market.

The Role of Carbon Credits:

To further incentivize emission reductions, carbon markets often incorporate the concept of carbon credits. A carbon credit represents one metric ton of carbon dioxide equivalent (CO_2e) emissions that have been reduced or removed from the atmosphere. These credits can be bought and sold, allowing organizations that have exceeded their emission reduction targets to sell their surplus credits to those who have not met their targets.

Benefits of Carbon Markets:

Carbon markets offer several benefits in the fight against climate change. Firstly, they provide a flexible and cost-effective approach to reducing emissions, as they allow for market forces to determine the most efficient ways to achieve emission reductions. Secondly, carbon markets promote innovation by encouraging the development and adoption of cleaner technologies. Lastly, they can generate revenue for governments, which can be reinvested in climate change mitigation and adaptation efforts.

Challenges and Considerations:

While carbon markets have shown promise, they are not without challenges. One key challenge is ensuring the accuracy and transparency of emissions reporting and verification. Additionally, there is a need to address concerns regarding the potential for market manipulation and the distributional impacts of carbon pricing on different sectors and communities.

Conclusion:

Introducing carbon markets as a response to climate change is a significant step towards achieving global emission reduction targets. By putting a price on carbon emissions and creating financial incentives for emission reductions, carbon markets can play a crucial role in transitioning to a low-carbon economy. However, it is important to address the challenges and considerations associated with carbon markets to ensure their effectiveness and fairness in achieving sustainable development goals.

Note: This chapter provided a general overview of carbon markets and their role in addressing climate change, but for a more comprehensive understanding, further research and analysis are recommended.

•●•

Chapter - 2

Dr. Chirag Bhimani

The Basics of Carbon Trading

2.1 Outlining The Fundamentals of Carbon Markets

Carbon markets play a crucial role in addressing the global challenge of climate change. They provide a mechanism for countries, organizations, and individuals to reduce their greenhouse gas emissions and contribute to a more sustainable future. This chapter aims to outline the fundamentals of carbon markets, including their purpose, key components, and how they function.

Understanding Carbon Markets:

Definition:

Carbon markets, also known as emissions trading systems or cap-and-trade systems, are market-based approaches designed to reduce greenhouse gas emissions. They create a financial incentive for entities to reduce their emissions by setting a limit (cap) on the total amount of emissions allowed and allowing the trading of emission allowances.

Purpose:

The primary purpose of carbon markets is to provide economic incentives for emission reductions. By putting a price on carbon, these markets encourage entities to invest in cleaner technologies, improve energy efficiency, and adopt sustainable practices. This helps in achieving emission reduction targets set by governments and international agreements.

Key Components of Carbon Markets:

Emission Allowances:

Emission allowances represent the right to emit a certain amount of greenhouse gases. These allowances are allocated to entities based on their emission targets or historical emissions. They can be bought, sold, or traded in the carbon market.

Cap and Compliance:

Carbon markets set a cap on the total amount of emissions allowed within a specific jurisdiction or sector. Entities are required to hold enough emission allowances to cover their emissions. Failure to comply with the cap results in penalties or additional obligations.

Trading Mechanism:

Carbon markets facilitate the trading of emission allowances between entities. This can occur through auctions, bilateral agreements, or on secondary markets. The price of allowances is determined by supply and demand dynamics, reflecting the cost of reducing emissions.

Functioning of Carbon Markets:

Allocation Methods:

Carbon markets employ different allocation methods for distributing emission allowances. These can include free allocation based on historical emissions, auctioning, or a combination of both. The chosen method depends on policy objectives and the specific context of the market.

Offsets and Credits:

Some carbon markets allow the use of offsets and credits to meet emission reduction obligations. Offsets represent emission reductions achieved outside the capped sectors, such as forestry projects. Credits, on the other hand, are generated from projects that reduce emissions within the capped sectors.

Monitoring, Reporting, and Verification:

To ensure the integrity of carbon markets, robust monitoring, reporting, and verification systems are essential. Entities are required to accurately measure and report their emissions, which are then verified by independent third parties. This ensures transparency and credibility in the market.

Conclusion:

Carbon markets are a vital tool in the fight against climate change. By creating economic incentives for emission reductions, they encourage entities to transition to cleaner and more sustainable practices. Understanding the fundamentals of carbon markets, including their purpose, key components, and functioning, is crucial for effective participation and decision-making in these markets. As the world continues to address the challenges of climate change, carbon markets will play an increasingly important role in achieving a low-carbon future.

2.2 Explaining The Different Types of Carbon Credits

In recent years, the issue of climate change has gained significant attention worldwide. As a result, there has been a growing interest in finding ways to reduce greenhouse gas emissions and mitigate the impact of human activities on the environment. One such approach is the use of carbon credits, which provide a mechanism for individuals and organizations to offset their carbon footprint. In this chapter, we will explore the different types of carbon credits and how they contribute to the overall goal of reducing carbon emissions.

Carbon Offsetting:
Carbon offsetting is a process that allows individuals or organizations to compensate for their carbon emissions by investing in projects that reduce or remove greenhouse gases from the atmosphere. These projects can include renewable energy initiatives, reforestation efforts, or energy efficiency improvements. Carbon credits are the units of measurement used to quantify the reduction or removal of greenhouse gases.

Verified Emission Reductions (VERs):
Verified Emission Reductions, also known as voluntary carbon credits, are generated through projects that are not regulated by any specific government or international body. These projects are typically undertaken voluntarily by organizations or individuals who wish to take responsibility for their carbon emissions. VERs are often used by companies as part of their corporate social responsibility initiatives or by individuals who want to offset their personal carbon footprint.

Certified Emission Reductions (CERs):

Certified Emission Reductions are carbon credits generated through projects that are regulated under the Clean Development Mechanism (CDM) of the United Nations Framework Convention on Climate Change (UNFCCC). The CDM allows developed countries to invest in emission reduction projects in developing countries as a way to meet their own emission reduction targets. CERs are issued for each ton of carbon dioxide equivalent (CO2e) reduced or removed by these projects.

Emission Reduction Units (ERUs):

Emission Reduction Units are carbon credits generated through projects that are regulated under the Joint Implementation (JI) mechanism of the UNFCCC. Similar to the CDM, the JI allows developed countries to invest in emission reduction projects in other developed countries. ERUs are issued for each ton of CO2e reduced or removed by these projects.

Compliance Carbon Credits:

Compliance carbon credits are generated through projects that are regulated by government bodies or international agreements. These credits are used by companies or countries to meet their legally binding emission reduction targets. Examples of compliance carbon credits include European Union Allowances (EUAs) under the European Union Emissions Trading System (EU ETS) and Certified Emission Reduction Units (CERs) under the Kyoto Protocol. Thus, we can see that Carbon credits play a crucial role in the global effort to combat climate change. By understanding the different types of carbon credits, individuals and organizations can make informed decisions about how to offset their carbon emissions effectively. Whether through voluntary or compliance-based initiatives, carbon credits provide a tangible way to contribute to the reduction of greenhouse gas emissions and create a more sustainable future for generations to come.

2.3 Detailing The Mechanisms of Emissions Trading Schemes (ETS) And Cap and Trade Systems

In recent years, the global community has recognized the urgent need to address climate change and reduce greenhouse gas emissions. One of the key strategies employed to achieve this goal is the implementation of emissions trading schemes (ETS) and cap and trade systems. This chapter aims to provide a comprehensive overview of these mechanisms, their underlying principles, and how they function to mitigate emissions.

Understanding Emissions Trading Schemes (ETS):

An emissions trading scheme, also known as a carbon market, is a market-based approach to controlling pollution. It sets a limit, or cap, on the total amount of emissions allowed within a specific jurisdiction or sector. This cap is then divided into individual allowances, which represent the right to emit a certain amount of greenhouse gases. These allowances can be bought, sold, or traded among participants in the scheme.

The Cap and Trade System:

Cap and trade is a specific type of emissions trading scheme that sets a cap on total emissions and allows participants to trade emission allowances. Under this system, a regulatory authority establishes the cap based on environmental targets and allocates a certain number of allowances to participants. These allowances can be freely traded in a secondary market, enabling companies to buy or sell allowances based on their emission needs.

Mechanisms of Emissions Trading Schemes

Allowance Allocation:

The process of allocating allowances is a crucial aspect of emissions trading schemes. There are various methods for determining how allowances are distributed, including free allocation, auctioning, and a combination of both. Free allocation involves granting allowances to participants based on historical emissions or other predetermined criteria. Auctioning, on the other hand, involves selling allowances to the highest bidder, generating revenue for the regulatory authority.

Compliance and Monitoring:

To ensure the effectiveness of emissions trading schemes, compliance and monitoring mechanisms are put in place. Participants are required to surrender a sufficient number of allowances to cover their emissions during a specified compliance period. Monitoring systems, such as emissions reporting and verification, are implemented to track and verify the accuracy of reported emissions.

Offsets and Banking:

Emissions trading schemes often allow for the use of offsets and banking. Offsets are credits generated from projects that reduce emissions outside the capped sector, such as renewable energy projects or reforestation initiatives. These offsets can be used to meet compliance obligations. Banking refers to the ability of participants to save unused allowances for future use, providing flexibility in managing emissions.

Advantages and Challenges:

Emissions trading schemes and cap and trade systems offer several advantages. They provide economic incentives for emission reductions, promote innovation, and allow for flexibility in meeting targets. However, challenges such as market manipulation, price volatility, and ensuring environmental integrity need to be addressed to ensure the long-term success of these mechanisms.

Conclusion:

Emissions trading schemes and cap and trade systems play a crucial role in mitigating greenhouse gas emissions. By setting a cap on total emissions and allowing for the trading of allowances, these mechanisms provide economic incentives for emission reductions. Understanding the mechanisms and intricacies of these systems is essential for policymakers, businesses, and individuals alike as we strive to combat climate change and create a sustainable future.

2.4 Analyzing The Key Players in The Carbon Trading Landscape

In recent years, the issue of climate change has gained significant attention worldwide. As governments and organizations strive to reduce greenhouse gas emissions, carbon trading has emerged as a crucial tool in the fight against climate change. Carbon trading allows companies to buy and sell carbon credits, creating a market-based approach to reducing emissions. In this chapter, we will analyze the key players in the carbon trading landscape, including governments, international organizations, and market participants.

Governments:

Governments play a vital role in shaping the carbon trading landscape. Many countries have implemented cap-and-trade systems or carbon pricing mechanisms to regulate emissions. These governments set emission reduction targets and allocate allowances to companies. They also establish the rules and regulations governing the carbon market, ensuring transparency and accountability. Examples of governments actively involved in carbon trading include the European Union, China, and California.

International Organizations:

International organizations play a crucial role in coordinating and facilitating carbon trading efforts on a global scale. The United Nations Framework Convention on Climate Change **(UNFCCC)** oversees the implementation of the Paris Agreement, which aims to limit global warming to well below 2 degrees Celsius. The UNFCCC provides a platform for countries to negotiate and collaborate on carbon trading initiatives. Additionally, the World Bank's Carbon Pricing Leadership Coalition (CPLC) promotes the adoption of carbon pricing policies worldwide.

Market Participants:

Market participants are the entities actively engaged in buying and selling carbon credits. These participants include companies, financial institutions, and carbon offset project developers. Companies that emit large amounts of greenhouse gases, such as power plants or industrial facilities, are required to purchase carbon credits to offset their emissions. Financial institutions, such as banks and investment firms, facilitate the trading of carbon credits by providing liquidity and financial services. Carbon offset project developers generate carbon credits by implementing projects that reduce emissions or remove carbon from the atmosphere.

Carbon Exchanges and Registries:

Carbon exchanges and registries serve as the platforms where carbon credits are traded and recorded. These entities provide the infrastructure and technology necessary for transparent and secure transactions. Examples of carbon exchanges include the European Energy Exchange (EEX), the Chicago Climate Exchange (CCX), and the California Carbon Market. Carbon registries, such as the Clean Development Mechanism (CDM) registry, track the issuance, transfer, and retirement of carbon credits, ensuring their integrity and traceability.

Verification and Certification Bodies:

Verification and certification bodies play a crucial role in ensuring the credibility and integrity of carbon credits. These independent organizations assess and verify emission reduction projects, ensuring that they meet the required standards and methodologies. Examples of verification and certification bodies include the Verified Carbon Standard (VCS), Gold Standard, and the American Carbon Registry (ACR). Their involvement provides confidence to market participants and ensures the transparency of the carbon trading process.

Conclusion:

Analyzing the key players in the carbon trading landscape reveals the complex and interconnected nature of this market. Governments, international organizations, market participants, exchanges, registries, and verification bodies all contribute to the functioning and effectiveness of carbon trading. Understanding the roles and responsibilities of these players is essential for policymakers, businesses, and individuals seeking to navigate the carbon market and contribute to global efforts in combating climate change.

Chapter - 3

International Carbon Market Mechanisms

3.1 Exploring The Architecture of International Carbon Markets

In recent years, the issue of climate change has gained significant attention worldwide. As countries strive to reduce greenhouse gas emissions and mitigate the impacts of global warming, international carbon markets have emerged as a crucial tool in the fight against climate change. This chapter aims to provide an overview of the architecture of international carbon markets, exploring their key components, mechanisms, and challenges.

Understanding Carbon Markets:

Carbon markets, also known as emissions trading systems, are designed to create economic incentives for reducing greenhouse gas emissions. They operate on the principle of putting a price on carbon, allowing entities to buy and sell emission allowances or credits. These markets provide a flexible and cost-effective approach to achieving emission reduction targets.

Types of Carbon Markets:

There are two main types of Carbon Markets: cap-and-trade systems and carbon offset markets. Cap-and-trade systems set a limit, or cap, on the total amount of emissions allowed within a specific jurisdiction. Tradable emission allowances are then allocated to entities, which can be bought, sold, or traded. Carbon offset markets, on the other hand, enable entities to invest in emission reduction projects to offset their own emissions.

International Carbon Market Mechanisms:

International carbon markets can be structured through various mechanisms. One prominent example is the Clean Development Mechanism (CDM) under the Kyoto Protocol, which allows developed countries to invest in emission reduction projects in developing countries. Another mechanism is the Paris Agreement's Article 6, which aims to establish a framework for international cooperation in carbon markets.

Challenges and Considerations:

While international carbon markets offer significant potential, they also face several challenges. One key challenge is ensuring environmental integrity, as the credibility and effectiveness of carbon markets rely on accurate measurement, reporting, and verification of emissions reductions. Additionally, issues such as market manipulation, double counting, and the distributional impacts of carbon pricing need to be carefully addressed.

Future Outlook and Conclusion:

The architecture of international carbon markets is continuously evolving as countries strive to enhance their climate change mitigation efforts. The establishment of robust and transparent market mechanisms is crucial for achieving global emission reduction targets. As technology advances and international cooperation strengthens, the potential for international carbon markets to play a significant role in addressing climate change becomes increasingly promising.

In conclusion, this chapter has provided an overview of the architecture of international carbon markets. By understanding the key components, mechanisms, and challenges associated with these markets, policymakers, businesses, and individuals can make informed decisions and contribute to the global effort to combat climate change

3.2 Evaluating the Compliance and Voluntary Carbon Markets

The global concern for climate change has led to the development of various mechanisms to reduce greenhouse gas emissions. Two prominent approaches are the compliance and voluntary carbon markets. This chapter aims to evaluate these markets, their effectiveness, and their role in mitigating climate change.

Understanding Compliance Carbon Markets:

Compliance carbon markets are regulatory systems established by governments to enforce emission reduction targets. These markets typically operate under a cap-and-trade or carbon tax framework. Companies are required to hold a certain number of emission allowances or pay a penalty for exceeding their allocated emissions. These markets aim to incentivize emission reductions by creating a financial value for carbon emissions.

Assessing the Effectiveness of Compliance Carbon Markets:

Evaluating the effectiveness of compliance carbon markets involves analyzing their ability to achieve emission reduction targets and promote sustainable practices. Key factors to consider include the stringency of the targets, the market design, and the level of participation by regulated entities. Additionally, the monitoring, reporting, and verification mechanisms play a crucial role in ensuring the integrity of these markets.

Evaluating Voluntary Carbon Markets:

Voluntary carbon markets, on the other hand, are marketplaces where individuals, organizations, or governments can voluntarily purchase carbon offsets or credits to compensate for their emissions. These markets are not regulated by governments and operate based on voluntary commitments. Participants in voluntary markets often seek to demonstrate their environmental responsibility or support projects that contribute to emission reductions.

Assessing the Credibility of Voluntary Carbon Markets:

Evaluating the credibility of voluntary carbon markets is essential to ensure that purchased offsets or credits represent real emission reductions. Key considerations include the transparency and robustness of project verification methodologies, the additionality of emission reductions, and the avoidance of double counting. Independent third-party certification schemes can enhance the credibility of voluntary carbon markets.

Comparing Compliance and Voluntary Carbon Markets:

When comparing compliance and voluntary carbon markets, several factors come into play. Compliance markets are typically more regulated and have legally binding emission reduction targets, while voluntary markets rely on voluntary commitments. Compliance markets often cover a broader range of sectors and have a higher level of oversight, whereas voluntary markets offer more flexibility and can support innovative projects.

Conclusion:

Evaluating the compliance and voluntary carbon markets is crucial to understanding their effectiveness in mitigating climate change. Compliance markets provide a regulatory framework to enforce emission reduction targets, while voluntary markets offer flexibility and support for additional emission reduction efforts. Both markets have their strengths and weaknesses, and a combination of both approaches may be necessary to achieve significant and sustainable emission reductions.

In conclusion, the evaluation of compliance and voluntary carbon markets requires careful consideration of their effectiveness, credibility, and role in addressing climate change. Continued research and improvement in market design and oversight will be essential to ensure the success of these markets in the future.

3.3 Examining The United Nations Framework Convention on Climate Change (UNFCCC) Initiatives, Such as The Clean Development Mechanism (CDM) and the Paris Agreement

The United Nations Framework Convention on Climate Change (UNFCCC) is an international treaty established in 1992 with the objective of addressing the global issue of climate change. Over the years, the UNFCCC has introduced various initiatives to combat climate change and promote sustainable development. This chapter aims to examine two significant initiatives under the UNFCCC: The Clean Development Mechanism (CDM) and the Paris Agreement.

The Clean Development Mechanism (CDM):

The Clean Development Mechanism (CDM) is a project-based mechanism established under the Kyoto Protocol, which is an international treaty under the UNFCCC. The CDM aims to assist developing countries in achieving sustainable development while reducing greenhouse gas emissions. It allows developed countries to invest in emission reduction projects in developing countries and receive certified emission reduction credits (CERs) in return.

Objectives and Benefits of the CDM:

The primary objective of the CDM is to promote sustainable development by encouraging the transfer of environmentally friendly technologies and practices to developing countries. By investing in emission reduction projects, developed countries can offset their own emissions and contribute to global emission reduction efforts. The CDM also provides financial and technological support to developing countries, helping them transition to low-carbon economies and achieve their sustainable development goals.

Challenges and Criticisms of the CDM:

While the CDM has been successful in promoting sustainable development and emission reduction, it has faced several challenges and criticisms. One major concern is the additionality criterion, which requires CDM projects to demonstrate that they would not have occurred without the financial support from developed countries. Ensuring the integrity of CDM projects and avoiding double counting of emission reductions has also been a challenge. Additionally, there have been concerns about the distribution of CDM projects, with some arguing that they disproportionately benefit certain regions or industries.

The Paris Agreement:

The Paris Agreement is a landmark international treaty adopted in 2015 under the UNFCCC. It aims to limit global warming to well below 2 degrees Celsius above pre-industrial levels and pursue efforts to limit the temperature increase to 1.5 degrees Celsius. The agreement sets out a framework for countries to enhance their climate actions and strengthen international cooperation.

Key Elements of the Paris Agreement:

The Paris Agreement emphasizes the importance of nationally determined contributions (NDCs), which are the climate actions that each country commits to undertake. It also establishes a transparency framework to enhance the understanding and tracking of countries' progress towards their climate goals. The agreement promotes financial and technological support to developing countries and encourages the mobilization of climate finance from various sources.

Implementation and Challenges of the Paris Agreement:

The implementation of the Paris Agreement involves regular reporting and review of countries' climate actions, as well as the global stocktaking process to assess collective progress towards the agreement's goals. However, challenges remain, including the need for increased ambition in countries' NDCs, the mobilization of adequate climate finance, and the effective implementation of adaptation measures.

Conclusion:

The UNFCCC initiatives, such as the Clean Development Mechanism (CDM) and the Paris Agreement, play crucial roles in addressing climate change and promoting sustainable development. While the CDM has facilitated emission reduction projects and technology transfer, the Paris Agreement provides a comprehensive framework for global climate action. However, challenges and criticisms exist for both initiatives, highlighting the need for continuous improvement and international cooperation in tackling the complex issue of climate change.

•●•

Chapter - 4

Carbon Market Instruments and Standards

4.1 Unveiling the Different Carbon Market Instruments and Their Peculiarities

As the global community intensifies its efforts to combat climate change, carbon markets have emerged as essential tools for regulating and reducing greenhouse gas emissions. These markets operate on the principle of putting a price on carbon, thereby creating economic incentives for businesses and nations to reduce their carbon footprint. Within the intricate landscape of carbon markets, various instruments play distinct roles, each with its own peculiarities and nuances.

Carbon Allowances:

Carbon allowances represent one of the foundational instruments within carbon markets. These are permits issued by regulatory authorities, setting a cap on the total amount of greenhouse gas emissions a company or entity is allowed to produce. Companies that emit below their allocated limit can sell their surplus allowances to those exceeding their limits. This establishes a dynamic marketplace where the cost of emitting carbon is determined by supply and demand forces.

Carbon Offsets:

In the quest for emissions reduction, carbon offsets provide an avenue for entities to compensate for their unavoidable emissions. These are credits generated by projects that remove or reduce emissions elsewhere. Projects may include reforestation initiatives, renewable energy projects, or methane capture programs. The peculiar nature of offsets lies in their ability to offer flexibility, allowing businesses to meet their emission reduction targets indirectly.

Cap-and-Trade Systems:

Cap-and-trade systems establish an overall emissions cap for a particular jurisdiction, with allowances distributed or auctioned among participating entities. This system allows for flexibility, enabling businesses to either reduce their emissions or purchase additional allowances. The peculiarity of cap-and-trade lies in its ability to facilitate emissions reduction while providing a market-driven approach that fosters innovation.

Carbon Taxes:

In contrast to cap-and-trade systems, carbon taxes directly impose a price on carbon emissions. Entities are taxed based on the amount of carbon dioxide they emit, creating a financial disincentive for excessive emissions. The simplicity of carbon taxes appeals to policymakers, but their effectiveness depends on setting the right price to drive meaningful emissions reductions without imposing undue economic burdens.

Carbon Reduction Commitment (CRC):

The CRC is a regulatory instrument that mandates organizations to report and reduce their carbon emissions. Unlike cap-and-trade systems, the CRC does not involve the direct trading of allowances. Instead, it focuses on mandatory emissions reporting and places a financial penalty on organizations failing to meet their reduction targets. The CRC's peculiarity lies in its emphasis on transparency and direct regulatory oversight.

Renewable Energy Certificates (RECs):

RECs are market-based instruments that certify the generation of renewable energy. Each certificate represents a specific amount of clean energy produced and can be traded separately from the actual electricity. The peculiarity of RECs lies in their ability to incentivize renewable energy production and consumption without directly regulating carbon emissions.

Challenges and Opportunities:

While these carbon market instruments offer promising avenues for emissions reduction, they are not without challenges. Ensuring environmental integrity, preventing market manipulation, and addressing issues of social equity are ongoing concerns. Nevertheless, as the world grapples with the urgency of climate action, these instruments provide valuable tools to transition towards a low-carbon future.

In the dynamic and evolving landscape of carbon markets, understanding the peculiarities of each instrument is crucial. As nations and businesses navigate this complex terrain, a thoughtful combination of these instruments may hold the key to achieving meaningful and sustainable emissions reductions on a global scale.

4.2 Demonstrating the Significance of Carbon Pricing and Its Methodologies

In the face of escalating climate change challenges, the adoption of carbon pricing has emerged as a critical strategy to internalize the social cost of carbon emissions. By assigning a monetary value to carbon, this approach seeks to incentivize the reduction of greenhouse gas emissions and promote the transition to a low-carbon economy. This chapter delves into the significance of carbon pricing and explores the methodologies employed to implement this transformative tool.

The Economic Rationale for Carbon Pricing:

Carbon pricing rests on the economic principle of internalizing externalities-ensuring that the costs of environmental damage caused by carbon emissions are reflected in the price of goods and services. This approach aligns economic incentives with environmental objectives, encouraging businesses to minimize their carbon footprint by incorporating the true cost of emissions into their decision-making processes.

Driving Innovation and Technological Advancement:

One of the key advantages of carbon pricing is its ability to stimulate innovation. As businesses face financial implications for high carbon emissions, they are incentivized to explore and adopt cleaner, more sustainable technologies. This not only contributes to a more environmentally friendly industrial landscape but also fosters the development of new markets for low-carbon products and services.

Market-Based Mechanisms:

Carbon pricing employs market-based mechanisms to allocate emission allowances or set a price on carbon. Cap-and-trade systems and carbon taxes are the two primary market-based approaches. Cap-and-trade establishes a fixed cap on emissions and allows trading of allowances, while carbon taxes directly impose a price on each unit of emitted carbon. These mechanisms provide flexibility for businesses to choose the most cost-effective path to emissions reduction.

Revenue Generation and Sustainable Finance:

The revenue generated from carbon pricing can be instrumental in funding sustainable initiatives. Governments can reinvest the proceeds into renewable energy projects, energy efficiency programs, and climate adaptation measures. Additionally, carbon pricing can contribute to the development of sustainable finance by creating opportunities for green investments and environmentally conscious financial instruments.

Social Equity and Environmental Justice:

While implementing carbon pricing, it is imperative to consider social equity and environmental justice. The burden of increased costs associated with carbon pricing should be distributed fairly to prevent disproportionate impacts on vulnerable communities. Transparent policies, revenue-sharing mechanisms, and targeted investments in disadvantaged areas can help ensure that the transition to a low-carbon economy is inclusive and just.

Global Cooperation and Emission Reduction Targets:

Carbon pricing is not confined to national borders. The establishment of a global carbon pricing framework encourages international cooperation in the fight against climate change. Harmonizing methodologies and creating linkages between different carbon markets can enhance efficiency and contribute to achieving collective emission reduction targets on a global scale.

Overcoming Challenges and Resistance:

Despite its potential benefits, the implementation of carbon pricing faces challenges, including political resistance, concerns about economic competitiveness, and the need for accurate carbon pricing methodologies. Policymakers must address these challenges through effective communication, stakeholder engagement, and continuous refinement of pricing mechanisms to ensure broad acceptance and success.

In conclusion, carbon pricing stands as a linchpin in the arsenal of strategies to combat climate change. By assigning a tangible value to carbon emissions, it provides a powerful economic tool to drive emissions reductions, foster innovation, and transition toward a sustainable, low-carbon future. Through careful design, international collaboration, and ongoing refinement, carbon pricing can play a pivotal role in addressing the urgent and complex challenges posed by global climate change.

4.3 Identifying Various Carbon Market Standards and Certifications:

The success of carbon markets relies not only on effective policies and instruments but also on robust standards and certifications that ensure transparency, credibility, and environmental integrity. In this chapter, we explore the diverse landscape of carbon market standards and certifications, shedding light on the frameworks that underpin the credibility and effectiveness of emissions reduction initiatives.

The Role of Standards in Carbon Markets:

Carbon market standards serve as benchmarks, providing a common set of rules and criteria to assess and validate emission reduction projects. These standards play a pivotal role in building trust among market participants, investors, and the public, ensuring that emission reductions are legitimate, additional, and contribute to sustainable development goals.

Gold Standard for the Global Goals:

The Gold Standard for the Global Goals is a widely recognized certification that goes beyond carbon mitigation, incorporating social and environmental co-benefits into project assessment. Developed by the Gold Standard Foundation, this standard ensures that emission reduction projects contribute to sustainable development, poverty reduction, and the achievement of global climate goals.

Verified Carbon Standard (VCS):

The Verified Carbon Standard (VCS) is a leading global standard for voluntary carbon offset projects. Administered by Verra, the VCS provides a robust framework for the measurement, monitoring, and verification of greenhouse gas emissions reductions. Projects adhering to VCS guidelines undergo a rigorous assessment to ensure the accuracy and credibility of their claimed emission reductions.

Climate, Community, and Biodiversity (CCB) Standards:

The Climate, Community, and Biodiversity (CCB) Standards, managed by the CCB Alliance, focus on projects that not only reduce emissions but also deliver significant co-benefits for local communities and biodiversity conservation. These standards emphasize the importance of ensuring that emission reduction activities contribute to broader sustainability objectives.

American Carbon Registry (ACR):

The American Carbon Registry (ACR) is a reputable standard primarily focused on the North American carbon market. ACR provides a rigorous framework for the registration and verification of greenhouse gas emissions reduction projects, with an emphasis on market transparency and environmental integrity.

Plan Vivo Standard:

The Plan Vivo Standard is designed for projects that engage local communities in developing countries. Administered by the Plan Vivo Foundation, this standard emphasizes community involvement, social equity, and sustainable development alongside measurable emissions reductions. It is particularly well-suited for projects that support rural livelihoods and empower local communities.

Social Carbon:

Social Carbon is a standard that places a strong emphasis on social considerations and community engagement in carbon offset projects. Developed by the Social Carbon Company, this standard ensures that projects not only reduce emissions but also contribute to social well-being, poverty alleviation, and community development.

Emerging Standards and Innovations:

The field of carbon market standards continues to evolve, with new standards and innovations emerging to address specific challenges and opportunities. These may include sector-specific standards, technology-focused certifications, or standards designed to facilitate the integration of nature-based solutions into carbon markets.

Challenges in Standardization:

While carbon market standards play a crucial role in ensuring the environmental integrity of emissions reduction projects, challenges persist. These may include the need for harmonization among different standards, addressing concerns related to additionality, and continually adapting to advancements in measurement and verification technologies.

The Future of Carbon Market Standards:

As carbon markets expand and evolve, the role of standards and certifications will become increasingly vital. The ongoing development and refinement of standards will be essential to build trust, facilitate cross-border trading, and ensure that carbon market mechanisms effectively contribute to global efforts to mitigate climate change.

In conclusion, the identification and adherence to robust carbon market standards and certifications are fundamental to the success and credibility of emission reduction initiatives. These frameworks provide the necessary assurance that carbon credits represent real and additional emissions reductions, fostering confidence among investors, businesses, and the broader public in the pursuit of a more sustainable and low-carbon future.

• ● •

Chapter - 5

Carbon Market Participants and Trading Strategies

5.1 Profiling the Major Players in Carbon Markets, Including Governments, Project Developers, and Financial Institutions

Carbon markets operate as dynamic ecosystems where various stakeholders play pivotal roles in shaping the landscape of emissions trading, offset projects, and sustainable finance. Understanding the key players is essential for comprehending the intricate web of relationships and influences within the carbon market. In this chapter, we profile the major players, including governments, project developers, and financial institutions.

Governments as Policy Drivers:

Governments are central figures in the carbon market, wielding regulatory power to establish and shape carbon pricing mechanisms. They set emission reduction targets, design policies and regulations, and create the frameworks for cap-and-trade systems, carbon taxes, and other market-based approaches. Governments also participate directly in the market, purchasing carbon credits to meet national emission reduction goals or offsetting their own emissions.

Project Developers and Offset Initiatives:

Project developers are instrumental in implementing emission reduction projects that generate carbon credits. These projects span a range of activities, including renewable energy generation, reforestation, methane capture, and energy efficiency. Project developers navigate the complexities of carbon market standards, ensuring that their initiatives meet rigorous criteria for additionality, permanence, and verifiability. They play a crucial role in the supply of carbon credits to the market.

Financial Institutions Driving Investment:

Financial institutions, including banks, investment funds, and carbon market participants, are key contributors to the growth and liquidity of carbon markets. They provide financing for emission reduction projects, facilitate the trading of carbon credits, and engage in sustainable finance initiatives. Financial institutions play a dual role, acting as both investors and intermediaries, channeling capital into projects that align with environmental, social, and governance (ESG) criteria.

Carbon Exchanges and Trading Platforms:

Carbon exchanges and trading platforms serve as the marketplaces where carbon credits are bought and sold. These platforms facilitate transactions, ensure market liquidity, and provide a transparent environment for participants. Notable examples include the European Union Emissions Trading System (EU ETS), the Chicago Climate Exchange (CCX), and the California Carbon Market. These exchanges connect buyers and sellers, enabling the efficient transfer of carbon assets.

International Organizations and Initiatives:

International organizations, such as the United Nations Framework Convention on Climate Change (UNFCCC) and its Kyoto Protocol, play a significant role in shaping the global carbon market landscape. They establish guidelines, standards, and mechanisms for international cooperation on emission reductions. Initiatives like the Clean Development Mechanism (CDM) and the Paris Agreement provide frameworks for cross-border collaboration and the exchange of emission reduction credits.

Non-Governmental Organizations (NGOs) and Advocacy Groups:

Non-governmental organizations and advocacy groups contribute to the carbon market by promoting transparency, accountability, and environmental sustainability. They monitor projects, advocate for strong standards, and engage in initiatives that ensure the equitable distribution of benefits and the protection of local communities. NGOs play a watchdog role, holding market participants accountable for their environmental and social commitments.

Corporations Embracing Carbon Neutrality:

Corporations, both large and small, are increasingly recognizing the importance of carbon neutrality in the face of climate change. Many corporations voluntarily engage in carbon markets to offset their emissions, meet sustainability goals, and enhance their environmental stewardship. Companies may invest in emission reduction projects, purchase carbon credits, or implement internal carbon pricing mechanisms to align their business practices with climate objectives.

Academia and Research Institutions:

Academic and research institutions contribute valuable insights to the carbon market through scientific research, policy analysis, and the development of innovative methodologies. They play a crucial role in advancing the understanding of climate change, carbon accounting, and the effectiveness of market-based mechanisms. Researchers contribute to the evolution of standards, methodologies, and best practices within the carbon market.

Challenges and Opportunities for Collaboration:

While these players each bring unique perspectives and contributions to the carbon market, challenges persist. Coordinating efforts among governments, project developers, financial institutions, and other stakeholders is essential for creating a cohesive and effective global response to climate change. Collaborative initiatives, information sharing, and the alignment of interests can unlock synergies and amplify the impact of individual efforts.

5.2 Analyzing Successful Carbon Trading Strategies Adopted by Renowned Organizations

In the dynamic landscape of carbon trading, certain organizations have emerged as pioneers, implementing successful strategies to navigate the complexities of carbon markets, reduce emissions, and contribute to sustainable development. This chapter delves into the diverse strategies employed by renowned organizations, examining their approaches to carbon trading and the lessons they offer for others seeking to embrace environmentally responsible practices.

Integration of Carbon Trading into Corporate Sustainability Goals:

Renowned organizations often view carbon trading as an integral component of their broader sustainability objectives. By aligning carbon trading strategies with corporate values and long-term sustainability goals, these organizations demonstrate a commitment to environmental responsibility. They go beyond mere compliance, actively seeking ways to reduce their carbon footprint and contribute to the transition to a low-carbon economy.

Diversification of Carbon Offset Projects:

Successful organizations recognize the importance of diversifying their carbon offset portfolio. Instead of relying solely on one type of project, such as renewable energy, they engage in a range of initiatives, including reforestation, methane capture, and energy efficiency. Diversification not only enhances the environmental impact of their efforts but also reduces risks associated with specific project types or geographical locations.

Leveraging Technology for Monitoring and Verification:

Advanced technologies play a crucial role in the success of carbon trading strategies. Renowned organizations invest in state-of-the-art monitoring and verification systems to ensure the accuracy and transparency of their emission reduction projects. Utilizing satellite imagery, sensors, and blockchain technology, they enhance the reliability of data, providing confidence to stakeholders and market participants.

Proactive Engagement with Carbon Market Standards:

Successful organizations actively engage with and contribute to the development of carbon market standards. They recognize the importance of adhering to robust standards, such as the Verified Carbon Standard (VCS) or the Gold Standard, and participate in their continual improvement. Proactive engagement with standards ensures that their carbon credits are widely accepted, fostering trust among investors and trading partners.

Collaborative Initiatives and Partnerships:

Renowned organizations understand the power of collaboration. They engage in partnerships with governments, NGOs, and other stakeholders to amplify the impact of their carbon trading strategies. Collaborative initiatives not only enhance the scale of emission reduction projects but also contribute to broader sustainability goals, including poverty alleviation, community development, and biodiversity conservation.

Internal Carbon Pricing Mechanisms:

Forward-thinking organizations implement internal carbon pricing mechanisms to internalize the cost of carbon emissions within their operations. By assigning a monetary value to carbon, they create financial incentives for departments and business units to reduce their emissions. This proactive approach not only contributes to emissions reduction targets but also fosters a culture of environmental responsibility within the organization.

Supply Chain Engagement:

Successful organizations extend their carbon trading strategies beyond their immediate operations, actively engaging with suppliers and partners throughout the supply chain. They work collaboratively to identify opportunities for emissions reduction, implement sustainable practices, and collectively contribute to the overall reduction of carbon footprint across the entire value chain.

Transparent Communication and Reporting:

Transparency is a hallmark of successful carbon trading strategies. Renowned organizations prioritize clear and accurate communication about their carbon reduction initiatives. They publish detailed reports on their emission reduction projects, carbon offset purchases, and progress toward sustainability goals. Transparent reporting not only builds trust among stakeholders but also sets a standard for industry best practices.

Continuous Innovation and Adaptation:

Leading organizations in carbon trading embrace a culture of continuous innovation. They invest in research and development, exploring new technologies, methodologies, and project types to stay ahead of the curve. By adapting to evolving market dynamics and emerging opportunities, these organizations position themselves as leaders in the transition to a sustainable, low-carbon future.

Lessons for Future Carbon Traders:

The success of renowned organizations in carbon trading provides valuable lessons for businesses, governments, and project developers entering the carbon market. The integration of carbon trading into broader sustainability goals, collaboration with diverse stakeholders, technological innovation, and a commitment to transparency are key elements that can guide the development of effective and impactful carbon trading strategies.

In conclusion, the analysis of successful carbon trading strategies employed by renowned organizations showcases the diverse approaches and best practices that contribute to the growth and effectiveness of carbon markets. As more entities join the global effort to mitigate climate change, these strategies offer insights and inspiration for creating meaningful and sustainable impact within the evolving landscape of carbon trading.

5.3 Discussing Risk Management and Mitigation Techniques in Carbon Trading

While carbon trading presents opportunities for emissions reduction and sustainable practices, it is not without risks. As organizations navigate the complexities of the carbon market, understanding and effectively managing risks are critical for ensuring the success and credibility of their carbon trading strategies. In this chapter, we delve into the various risks associated with carbon trading and explore techniques for risk management and mitigation.

Market Price Volatility:

Risk: Carbon credit prices can be subject to volatility influenced by regulatory changes, geopolitical events, and market dynamics.

Mitigation Techniques:

Diversification: Maintain a diversified portfolio of carbon credits across different projects and market mechanisms to spread risk.

Hedging Strategies: Employ financial instruments like futures or options to hedge against adverse price movements.

Stay Informed: Regularly monitor and stay informed about market developments, policy changes, and global events that may impact carbon prices.

Regulatory and Policy Risks:

Risk: Changes in government policies and regulations can significantly impact the value and market acceptance of carbon credits.

Mitigation Techniques:

Policy Advocacy: Engage in advocacy efforts to influence and shape favorable policies that support the carbon market.

Diversify Project Types: Invest in a variety of emission reduction projects to reduce dependence on a specific policy or regulatory framework.

Additionality and Permanence Risks:

Risk: The concept of additionality (ensuring that emissions reductions are beyond business-as-usual) and permanence (the risk of emissions being released after a project ends) poses challenges to the integrity of carbon credits.

Mitigation Techniques:

Robust Project Design: Implement rigorous project design and development processes that adhere to recognized standards, ensuring the highest level of additionality.

Insurance Mechanisms: Explore insurance options or risk-sharing mechanisms to address the permanence risk, such as forest carbon insurance for reforestation projects.

Methodological Risks:

Risk: Inaccuracies or uncertainties in the methodologies used for measuring and verifying emissions reductions can undermine the credibility of carbon credits.

Mitigation Techniques:

Continuous Monitoring: Implement advanced monitoring technologies and systems to enhance the accuracy of data collection.

Independent Verification: Engage independent third-party verifiers to validate emissions reductions and ensure compliance with established standards.

Reputational Risks:

Risk: Negative public perception or stakeholder backlash due to real or perceived issues with the environmental and social integrity of carbon offset projects.

Mitigation Techniques:

Transparent Communication: Maintain transparent and accurate communication about the organization's carbon trading activities, including successes, challenges, and ongoing initiatives.

Stakeholder Engagement: Actively engage with stakeholders, including local communities, NGOs, and the public, to address concerns and build trust.

Project Implementation Risks:

Risk: Delays, cost overruns, or technical challenges during the implementation of emission reduction projects.

Mitigation Techniques:

Thorough Due Diligence: Conduct comprehensive due diligence before initiating projects to identify and address potential implementation challenges.

Contingency Planning: Develop contingency plans to address unforeseen issues and minimize the impact on project timelines and budgets.

Legal and Contractual Risks:

Risk: Legal and contractual issues, such as disputes over project ownership, liability, or contractual obligations, can pose significant risks to carbon trading initiatives.

Mitigation Techniques:

Clear Contracts: Develop clear and legally robust contracts that outline the rights, responsibilities, and obligations of all parties involved.

Legal Expertise: Seek legal advice and expertise to navigate complex contractual arrangements and potential legal challenges.

Currency and Exchange Rate Risks:

Risk: For organizations involved in international carbon trading, currency fluctuations and exchange rate risks can impact the financial returns of carbon credit transactions.

Mitigation Techniques:

Currency Hedging: Use financial instruments, such as currency hedges, to mitigate the impact of currency fluctuations.

Diversified Currency Transactions: Engage in transactions in multiple currencies to spread the risk associated with exchange rate fluctuations.

Technological Risks:

Risk: Reliance on technology for monitoring, verification, and data management introduces the risk of technological failures, cybersecurity threats, or data breaches.

Mitigation Techniques:

Cybersecurity Measures Implement robust cybersecurity measures to protect sensitive data and prevent unauthorized access.

Backup Systems: Establish backup systems and protocols to ensure data integrity and continuity in the event of technological failures.

Continuous Monitoring and Adaptation:

Risk: The carbon market is dynamic, and risks can evolve over time. Failing to adapt to changing circumstances can expose organizations to new and unforeseen risks.

Mitigation Techniques:

Continuous Risk Assessment: Regularly assess and reassess risks associated with carbon trading, considering changes in market conditions, regulations, and project performance.

Agile Strategies: Adopt agile strategies that allow for quick adjustments to risk mitigation measures based on the evolving landscape of the carbon market.

In conclusion, effective risk management and mitigation are essential components of successful carbon trading strategies. By identifying, understanding, and proactively addressing various risks, organizations can navigate the complexities of the carbon market, enhance the credibility of their initiatives, and contribute to the global effort to mitigate climate change in a sustainable and responsible manner.

•●•

Chapter - 6

Dr. Chirag Bhimani

Investment Opportunities in Carbon Markets

6.1 Highlighting the Potential Investment Avenues Within Carbon Markets

As the global community intensifies efforts to address climate change, carbon markets have emerged as crucial instruments for fostering sustainable development and reducing greenhouse gas emissions. In this chapter, we delve into the various investment opportunities within carbon markets, exploring the potential avenues that investors can explore to contribute to environmental goals while generating financial returns.

Carbon Offsetting Projects:

One of the primary investment avenues within carbon markets is supporting carbon offsetting projects. These projects, such as reforestation initiatives, renewable energy developments, and methane capture programs, offer investors the opportunity to offset their own carbon footprint by investing in projects that reduce or remove greenhouse gas emissions.

Investors can explore partnerships with organizations involved in certified emission reduction (CER) projects under mechanisms like the Clean Development Mechanism (CDM) or the Gold Standard. These initiatives not only contribute to carbon neutrality but also support sustainable development goals.

Carbon Allowance Trading:

Carbon allowance trading, often conducted through emissions trading systems (ETS), provides another avenue for investment. Companies subject to emissions caps can buy and sell carbon allowances, creating a market where emissions reductions translate into financial value. Investors can engage in trading platforms, facilitating transactions and benefiting from market dynamics.

Understanding regional and international compliance markets, such as the European Union Emissions Trading System (EU ETS) or emerging markets like China's national ETS, is crucial for investors seeking to capitalize on allowance trading opportunities.

Climate-focused Investment Funds:

Climate-focused investment funds offer a diversified approach to carbon market investments. These funds pool capital from various investors to support a portfolio of projects and initiatives aimed at mitigating climate change. Such funds may invest in a range of sectors, including renewable energy, energy efficiency, and sustainable forestry.

Investors can explore opportunities with established climate-focused funds or consider creating specialized funds tailored to specific environmental objectives or geographic regions.

Green Bonds and Climate Finance Instruments:

The issuance of green bonds has gained traction as a means of financing environment-friendly projects. Investors can participate in these fixed-income securities, with the proceeds dedicated to projects with clear environmental benefits. Furthermore, climate finance instruments, including sustainability-linked bonds and loans, present innovative investment avenues tied to environmental performance metrics.

Understanding the criteria and standards set by organizations like the Climate Bonds Initiative is essential for investors looking to navigate the green bond market effectively.

Technology and Innovation Investments:

Investors keen on driving technological advancements within the carbon markets can explore opportunities in climate tech and innovation. These include investments in carbon capture and storage technologies, sustainable transportation solutions, and advancements in renewable energy.

Venture capital firms, private equity, and strategic partnerships with research institutions are potential avenues for investors looking to support and benefit from technological innovations in carbon mitigation.

Highlighting the potential investment avenues within carbon markets underscores the dual benefit of addressing climate change while creating profitable and sustainable investment portfolios. Investors are encouraged to assess risks thoroughly, align with reputable partners, and stay informed about evolving market dynamics to make informed decisions in this rapidly evolving space. As the global commitment to carbon reduction intensifies, the investment landscape within carbon markets is likely to expand, offering new opportunities for environmentally conscious investors.

6.2 Evaluating the Financial Value of Carbon Credits and Their Market Trends

In the dynamic landscape of carbon markets, understanding the financial value of carbon credits is crucial for investors seeking to navigate and capitalize on emerging opportunities. This chapter delves into the methodologies for evaluating the financial worth of carbon credits, examining market trends that influence their value and exploring key factors that contribute to market dynamics.

Valuation Metrics for Carbon Credits:

Evaluating the financial value of carbon credits requires a comprehensive understanding of the valuation metrics employed within the carbon market. Key metrics include the type of carbon credit (e.g. Certified Emission Reductions-CERs, Verified Carbon Units-VCUs), project-specific considerations, and the prevailing market price for carbon. Investors should consider the additionality, permanence, and verifiability of emissions reduction projects, as these factors impact the credibility and value of the associated carbon credits.

Regional Disparities and Market Trends:

Carbon credit markets exhibit regional disparities influenced by regulatory frameworks, market maturity, and governmental policies. Analyzing market trends across different regions allows investors to identify emerging opportunities and potential risks.

For example, the European Union Emissions Trading System (EU ETS) has historically been a major driver of carbon credit demand, influencing prices and market dynamics. Understanding such regional nuances is essential for making informed investment decisions.

Market Liquidity and Price Volatility:

Carbon credit markets, like any commodity market, experience fluctuations in liquidity and price volatility. Investors should be aware of factors contributing to these fluctuations, including regulatory changes, geopolitical events, and shifts in global demand for emissions reductions.

Tracking historical price trends and engaging with market analysts can help investors anticipate and respond to market dynamics, ensuring effective risk management.

Carbon Market Innovations:

Innovations within carbon markets, such as the introduction of new market mechanisms and compliance regimes, significantly impact the financial value of carbon credits. Investors should stay informed about developments in market infrastructure, including the potential expansion of cap-and-trade systems, the establishment of new carbon pricing initiatives, and advancements in standardized methodologies for measuring emissions reductions.

Investing in alignment with evolving market innovations allows investors to capitalize on emerging opportunities and position themselves strategically within the market.

Corporate and Social Responsibility Impact:

Increasingly, businesses and investors are recognizing the value of carbon credits as tools for corporate social responsibility (CSR) and sustainable investment. The financial worth of carbon credits is often influenced by companies' commitments to achieve carbon neutrality and meet sustainability targets. As consumer and investor awareness grows, businesses integrating carbon credit utilization into their sustainability strategies may experience enhanced market value and reputational benefits.

Evaluating the financial value of carbon credits requires a nuanced understanding of diverse factors, ranging from project-specific considerations to global market trends. Investors operating in carbon markets should continuously monitor regulatory developments, regional disparities, and market innovations to make informed decisions that align with financial goals and environmental objectives. As the carbon market landscape evolves, staying adaptable and well-informed is paramount for maximizing financial returns and contributing to a sustainable future.

6.3 Unraveling the Challenges and Opportunities in Green Finance and Impact Investing

As global awareness of environmental issues rises, green finance and impact investing have gained prominence as vehicles for aligning financial objectives with sustainable and socially responsible outcomes. In this chapter, we explore the challenges and opportunities within the realms of green finance and impact investing, providing insights for investors navigating this evolving landscape.

Challenges in Green Finance:

Regulatory Complexity:

Navigating the regulatory landscape in green finance poses a substantial challenge. Varied and evolving standards for green investments can create uncertainty for investors. Understanding and complying with different national and international regulations is essential for ensuring the integrity of green finance initiatives.

Measurement and Reporting Standards:

Accurate measurement and reporting of environmental impacts remain a challenge. Establishing standardized metrics for assessing the environmental and social performance of green investments is essential for providing transparency and comparability, yet achieving consensus on these metrics is an ongoing challenge.

Risk Perception and Mitigation:

Perceived risks in green finance, including policy and regulatory risks, can hinder broader adoption. Investors may be cautious due to uncertainties surrounding the long-term viability of green technologies or evolving government policies. Developing effective risk mitigation strategies is crucial for encouraging more significant investments in green projects.

Opportunities in Green Finance:

Growing Market Demand:

The increasing global awareness of environmental issues has created a growing market demand for green and sustainable investments. Opportunities abound for investors to capitalize on this demand by supporting renewable energy projects, sustainable agriculture, and other environmentally friendly initiatives.

Innovation and Technology Advancements:

Green finance benefits from ongoing innovations and advancements in technology. Investments in renewable energy, energy efficiency, and sustainable technologies offer investors the chance to participate in cutting-edge developments while contributing to the transition to a low-carbon economy.

Socially Responsible Investing (SRI):

The rise of socially responsible investing provides an avenue for investors to align their financial goals with ethical considerations. SRI strategies integrate environmental, social, and governance (ESG) criteria, allowing investors to support businesses that prioritize sustainability and positive societal impact.

Impact Investing:

Definition and Scope:

Impact investing seeks to generate positive social and environmental impact alongside financial returns. This approach goes beyond traditional philanthropy by actively investing in businesses and projects that contribute to sustainable development goals.

Diversification of Impact Investment Portfolios:

Investors have the opportunity to diversify their portfolios by allocating funds to impact investments across various sectors. These may include affordable housing, clean energy, healthcare, and education. Diversification not only mitigates risks but also broadens the positive societal impact of the investment.

Measuring Impact:

Measuring the impact of investments is a complex but integral aspect of impact investing. Investors should seek standardized metrics to assess the social and environmental outcomes of their investments. This includes metrics related to job creation, carbon reduction, and improvements in community well-being.

Thus, Green finance and impact investing present a dual challenge and opportunity landscape. While challenges such as regulatory complexity and risk perception persist, the growing market demand, technological advancements, and the potential for positive societal impact create a compelling case for investors to explore and contribute to these sustainable and impactful investment avenues. Adapting to changing landscapes, adopting standardized measurement practices, and embracing

innovation will be key for investors seeking to navigate the complexities and maximize the opportunities in green finance and impact investing.

•●•

Chapter - 7

Carbon Market Regulations and Policies

7.1 Delving into the Regulatory Frameworks Governing Carbon Markets Worldwide

As the importance of addressing climate change grows, regulatory frameworks play a pivotal role in shaping and governing carbon markets globally. In this chapter, we explore the diverse regulatory structures and mechanisms that countries and regions have implemented to manage and incentivize emissions reductions. Understanding these frameworks is essential for participants in carbon markets to navigate compliance, seize opportunities, and contribute to a sustainable future.

The Kyoto Protocol and the Clean Development Mechanism (CDM):

The Kyoto Protocol, adopted in 1997, laid the foundation for international efforts to combat climate change. Under its mechanisms, the Clean Development Mechanism (CDM) allowed developed countries to invest in emissions reduction projects in developing nations. CDM credits, known as Certified Emission Reductions (CERs), became tradable assets within the international carbon market.

Evolution and Legacy:

While the Kyoto Protocol's first commitment period concluded in 2012, the CDM's legacy persists. Understanding the evolution of the CDM and its lessons learned informs the design of subsequent regulatory frameworks and mechanisms.

Paris Agreement and Nationally Determined Contributions (NDCs):

The Paris Agreement, adopted in 2015, represents a landmark global commitment to limit global warming. Nationally Determined Contributions (NDCs) are central to this framework, outlining each country's voluntary emissions reduction targets and strategies. The Agreement emphasizes market mechanisms as tools for achieving these targets.

Article 6:

Article 6 of the Paris Agreement specifically addresses cooperative approaches, including international carbon markets. It provides a foundation for countries to engage in emissions trading, sustainable development mechanisms, and other market-driven initiatives.

Regional and National Carbon Pricing Initiatives:

Beyond international agreements, many countries and regions have implemented their own carbon pricing initiatives, reflecting a diversity of approaches.

European Union Emissions Trading System (EU ETS):

The EU ETS, established in 2005, is one of the world's largest cap-and-trade systems. It covers various industries, encouraging emissions reductions through market-based mechanisms. The system's success and challenges serve as a reference for other regions.

China's Emission Trading Systems:

China, a key player in global emissions, has been developing regional emissions trading systems with plans to establish a national system. Understanding China's evolving approach is critical for assessing future dynamics in the carbon market landscape.

Voluntary Carbon Markets and Standards:

Voluntary carbon markets, outside of regulatory requirements, have gained momentum as businesses and individuals seek to address their carbon footprints.

Verified Carbon Standard (VCS) and Gold Standard:

The VCS and Gold Standard are prominent voluntary carbon market standards, ensuring the credibility and quality of emissions reduction projects. Investors and organizations involved in voluntary markets often adhere to these standards to demonstrate their commitment to environmental integrity.

Hence, delving into the regulatory frameworks governing carbon markets worldwide reveals a complex and evolving landscape. From international agreements like the Kyoto Protocol and Paris Agreement to regional and national initiatives, the regulatory frameworks shape the incentives, constraints, and opportunities within the carbon market. As these frameworks continue to evolve, market participants must stay informed and adapt to new regulations, ensuring that their strategies align with both environmental objectives and compliance requirements.

7.2 Examining the Role of National and Regional Policies in Promoting Carbon Trading

National and regional policies play a pivotal role in shaping the landscape of carbon trading, influencing market dynamics and providing a framework for emissions reduction efforts. In this chapter, we delve into the diverse policies enacted by countries and regions to foster carbon trading, examining how these initiatives contribute to both environmental sustainability and economic development.

Cap-and-Trade Systems:

Cap-and-trade systems represent a cornerstone of national and regional policies promoting carbon trading. These systems establish a cap on total allowable emissions and allocate or auction emission allowances among regulated entities, allowing them to buy or sell allowances as needed.

European Union Emissions Trading System (EU ETS):

The EU ETS, a flagship cap-and-trade system, covers various industries across European Union member states. Its success in incentivizing emissions reductions while fostering economic growth serves as a model for other regions.

Regional Greenhouse Gas Initiative (RGGI) in the United States:

The RGGI, a cap-and-trade initiative in the northeastern United States, has demonstrated the effectiveness of regional collaboration in addressing emissions. Its experiences offer valuable insights for other subnational jurisdictions considering similar approaches.

Carbon Taxation:

Carbon taxation represents another policy tool wherein a tax is levied on the carbon content of fossil fuels or directly on greenhouse gas emissions. This approach incentivizes emitters to reduce their carbon footprint and provides revenue for climate-related initiatives.

British Columbia's Carbon Tax:

British Columbia's revenue-neutral carbon tax is frequently cited as a successful implementation of carbon pricing. The province's experience showcases how carbon taxation can drive emissions reductions without compromising economic growth.

Renewable Energy Standards and Credits:

Policies promoting renewable energy generation contribute significantly to carbon trading dynamics. Renewable energy standards mandate a certain percentage of energy production from renewable sources, while renewable energy credits create a market for trading these attributes.

Renewable Portfolio Standards (RPS) in the United States:

Various U.S. states have implemented Renewable Portfolio Standards, requiring a specified percentage of electricity to be generated from renewable sources. This approach fosters the development of renewable energy projects and creates tradable credits.

Sustainable Development Initiatives:

National and regional policies often integrate carbon trading within broader sustainable development initiatives. These policies aim to align economic growth with environmental stewardship.

South Africa's Carbon Tax and Sustainable Development Goals:

South Africa's carbon tax, implemented alongside sustainable development goals, exemplifies how a country can address carbon emissions while promoting social and economic development.

International Cooperation and Linking of Markets:

Countries and regions increasingly explore opportunities for international cooperation and market linkage to enhance the effectiveness of carbon trading.

California-Quebec Cap-and-Trade Linkage:

The linkage between California and Quebec's cap-and-trade systems exemplifies cross-border collaboration. By linking markets, jurisdictions can optimize the allocation of emissions allowances and facilitate cost-effective emissions reductions.

Examining the role of national and regional policies in promoting carbon trading underscores the diverse approaches adopted by jurisdictions worldwide. From cap-and-trade systems to carbon taxation and renewable energy standards, these policies not only drive emissions reductions but also shape the development of robust and sustainable carbon markets. As countries continue to refine their strategies, international collaboration and shared learning will be instrumental in advancing the global transition to a low-carbon economy.

7.3 Assessing the Potential Impact of Future Regulations on Carbon Markets

The evolution of carbon markets is intricately linked to the development and amendment of regulations governing emissions and sustainability. In this chapter, we explore the dynamic landscape of potential future regulations and their probable impacts on carbon markets, offering insights into how regulatory changes may shape the future of emissions trading.

Strengthening Emission Reduction Targets:

As the global commitment to combating climate change intensifies, one of the foreseeable trends in future regulations is the strengthening of emission reduction targets. Nations and regions are likely to revisit and enhance their commitments under international agreements, such as the Paris Agreement, potentially accelerating the demand for emissions reductions and carbon trading mechanisms.

Impact on Market Dynamics:

The intensification of emission reduction targets would likely spur increased participation in carbon markets, driving demand for carbon credits and influencing market prices. Investors and businesses should anticipate potential shifts in market dynamics as a result of more ambitious regulatory frameworks.

Expansion of Cap-and-Trade Systems:

Countries and regions with existing cap-and-trade systems may explore expanding the coverage of these mechanisms to include additional sectors or greenhouse gases. Such expansions aim to further incentivize emissions reductions across a broader spectrum of economic activities.

Market Growth and Integration:

The expansion of cap-and-trade systems can lead to market growth and increased integration. This could foster more extensive collaboration between jurisdictions, encouraging the development of linked markets and the establishment of a more interconnected global carbon market.

Implementation of Carbon Border Adjustment Mechanisms:

The concept of Carbon Border Adjustment Mechanisms (CBAM) is gaining traction as a means to address carbon leakage and ensure a level playing field for industries subject to carbon pricing. Future regulations may see the introduction of CBAM, imposing carbon-related tariffs on imported goods based on their embedded carbon footprint.

Implications for Global Trade:

The implementation of CBAM has potential implications for global trade, affecting industries in regions with varying carbon pricing mechanisms. Investors and businesses engaged in international trade should monitor developments in CBAM regulations and assess the associated risks and opportunities.

Integration of Nature-Based Solutions:

Future regulations may increasingly focus on integrating nature-based solutions, such as afforestation, reforestation, and sustainable land use practices, into carbon trading frameworks. This approach aligns with broader climate goals and emphasizes the role of natural ecosystems in sequestering carbon.

Market Opportunities in Nature-Based Credits:

Investors with an eye on the future may explore opportunities in nature-based credits, as regulations emphasizing the integration of such solutions could drive demand for projects that enhance carbon sequestration through sustainable land use practices.

Advancements in Methodologies and Measurement Standards:

To enhance the accuracy and credibility of carbon markets, future regulations may focus on advancing methodologies for measuring emissions reductions and establishing standardized reporting frameworks. This evolution aims to provide greater transparency and comparability across different projects and regions.

Impacts on Project Development:

As measurement standards advance, project developers may need to adapt their methodologies to meet evolving regulatory requirements. Investors should stay informed about these changes to ensure the continued integrity and quality of their carbon credit portfolios.

Thus, assessing the potential impact of future regulations on carbon markets is a complex yet essential task for investors and market participants. By anticipating regulatory trends related to emission reduction targets, market expansions, border adjustments, nature-based solutions, and measurement standards, stakeholders can position themselves strategically within the evolving carbon market landscape. As regulatory frameworks continue to evolve, a proactive and adaptive approach will be key to navigating the challenges and seizing opportunities presented by the dynamic future of carbon markets.

Chapter - 8

Case Studies and Success Stories

8.1 Showcasing Real-World Case Studies of Successful Carbon Market Projects

In this chapter, we delve into real-world case studies to showcase the diversity and success of carbon market projects. These projects exemplify the positive impact of emissions reduction initiatives, providing valuable insights for investors, businesses, and policymakers looking to navigate and contribute to the evolving landscape of carbon markets.

Renewable Energy Projects:

Wind Energy in Denmark:

Denmark's commitment to renewable energy is underscored by its successful wind energy projects. By investing in wind power infrastructure, Denmark has significantly reduced its reliance on fossil fuels and positioned itself as a global leader in renewable energy production.

Solar Power in India:

India's ambitious solar power initiatives demonstrate the transformative potential of carbon market projects. Through the implementation of large-scale solar projects, India has not only reduced carbon emissions but has also enhanced energy access, contributing to sustainable development.

Reforestation and Afforestation Initiatives:

Costa Rica's PES Program:

Costa Rica's Payment for Ecosystem Services (PES) program stands as a pioneering example of successful afforestation and reforestation. By financially incentivizing landowners to preserve and restore forests, Costa Rica has achieved a significant increase in forest cover, sequestering carbon and preserving biodiversity.

The Great Green Wall in Africa:

The Great Green Wall initiative, spanning multiple African countries, focuses on combating desertification and land degradation through afforestation. This project not only contributes to carbon sequestration but also addresses socio-economic challenges by creating jobs and promoting sustainable land use practices.

Methane Capture and Waste Management:

Landfill Gas-to-Energy in Brazil:

Brazil's landfill gas-to-energy projects exemplify the dual benefits of methane capture and sustainable energy production. By converting landfill gases into electricity, Brazil has reduced methane emissions, mitigated environmental impacts, and generated clean energy for communities.

Biogas from Agricultural Waste in Germany:

Germany's success in harnessing biogas from agricultural waste illustrates the potential of carbon market projects in waste management. By utilizing organic waste for biogas production, Germany has not only reduced methane emissions but has also created a renewable energy source.

Energy Efficiency and Industrial Projects:

Energy Efficiency in Sweden:

Sweden's commitment to energy efficiency is showcased through innovative projects in industries such as manufacturing and transportation. By adopting cutting- edge technologies and sustainable practices, Sweden has reduced carbon emissions while maintaining economic growth.

Cogeneration in the Netherlands:

The Netherlands' successful implementation of cogeneration, or combined heat and power (CHP), highlights the role of industrial projects in carbon markets. Cogeneration systems enhance energy efficiency by simultaneously producing electricity and useful heat, resulting in lower emissions per unit of energy produced.

International Collaboration and Market Linkage:

California-Quebec Cap-and-Trade Linkage:

The linkage between California and Quebec's cap-and-trade systems exemplifies successful international collaboration. By creating a joint carbon market, these jurisdictions have optimized emissions reductions, encouraged innovation, and facilitated cost-effective compliance.

Joint Crediting Mechanism (JCM) in Asia:

The Joint Crediting Mechanism, implemented in various Asian countries, promotes collaborative emissions reduction projects. Through technology transfer and shared expertise, participating nations have successfully reduced emissions while fostering sustainable development.

The real-world case studies presented in this chapter underscore the diversity and success of carbon market projects globally. From renewable energy initiatives to reforestation programs and innovative waste management projects, these cases demonstrate the potential of market-driven solutions to address climate change and achieve sustainable development goals. By drawing inspiration from these success stories, stakeholders can gain valuable insights into effective strategies and best practices for navigating and contributing to the dynamic landscape of carbon markets.

8.2 Drawing Lessons from These Cases to Inspire and Encourage Future Market Participants

In this section, we distill valuable lessons from the real-world case studies presented in the previous chapter. These lessons are intended to inspire and encourage future market participants, providing insights into successful strategies and practices within carbon markets. By examining the achievements of these projects, we aim to foster a deeper understanding of the opportunities and challenges inherent in emissions reduction initiatives.

Lesson 1: Integration of Sustainability and Economic Growth

Key Takeaway: Successful carbon market projects consistently demonstrate that environmental sustainability and economic growth are not mutually exclusive. In cases such as Denmark's wind energy projects and Sweden's focus on energy efficiency, the integration of sustainable practices has not only reduced carbon emissions but has also contributed to economic development. Future market participants are encouraged to explore projects that align with both environmental and economic goals, ensuring a balanced and resilient approach.

Lesson 2: Collaborative International Initiatives

Key Takeaway: The success of collaborative international initiatives, exemplified by the California-Quebec cap-and-trade linkage and the Joint Crediting Mechanism in Asia, underscores the importance of global cooperation. Future market participants should actively seek opportunities for collaboration, knowledge sharing, and technology transfer across borders. By engaging in joint efforts, countries and regions can optimize their emissions reduction strategies and achieve more significant environmental impact.

Lesson 3: Incentivizing Sustainable Practices Through Financial Mechanisms

Key Takeaway: Financial mechanisms, such as Costa Rica's Payment for Ecosystem Services (PES) program, play a crucial role in incentivizing sustainable practices. Future market participants should explore innovative financing models that reward positive environmental outcomes. The integration of financial incentives not only attracts project participation but also ensures the long-term viability and success of emissions reduction initiatives.

Lesson 4: Flexibility and Adaptability in Market Mechanisms

Key Takeaway: The adaptability of market mechanisms is evident in the success of cap-and-trade systems and the expansion of renewable energy standards. Future market participants should recognize the importance of flexibility in regulatory frameworks and market structures. This adaptability allows for the evolution of carbon markets over time, accommodating changing circumstances and advancing environmental objectives.

Lesson 5: Technology and Innovation as Catalysts

Key Takeaway: Technological innovation, as seen in Germany's use of biogas from agricultural waste and advancements in Sweden's industrial projects, serves as a catalyst for emissions reduction. Future market participants should actively seek and invest in cutting-edge technologies that enhance energy efficiency and reduce carbon intensity. Embracing innovation ensures the continual improvement and competitiveness of carbon market projects.

Lesson 6: Balancing Carbon Reduction with Social and Economic Benefits

Key Takeaway: Projects such as the Great Green Wall in Africa showcase the importance of balancing carbon reduction efforts with social and economic benefits. Future market participants are encouraged to adopt holistic approaches that address both environmental and socio-economic challenges. This ensures that emissions reduction initiatives contribute positively to local communities, fostering a broader impact beyond carbon mitigation.

The lessons drawn from these real-world case studies serve as a source of inspiration for future market participants. By learning from the successes and challenges of diverse carbon market projects, stakeholders can develop informed strategies, anticipate potential pitfalls, and contribute meaningfully to the global effort to combat climate change. As the carbon market landscape continues to evolve, the collective wisdom derived from these lessons will play a pivotal role in shaping sustainable and impactful emissions reduction initiatives.

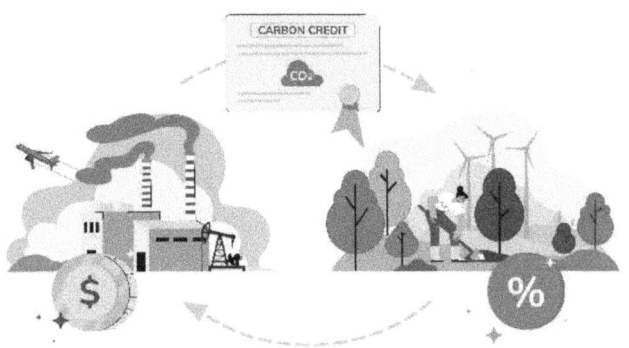

Chapter - 9

Dr. Chirag Bhimani

Carbon Market Outlook And Future Trends

9.1 Presenting an Overview of The Current State of Global Carbon Markets

As the global community intensifies efforts to address climate change, carbon markets play a central role in incentivizing emissions reductions and fostering sustainable practices. This chapter provides an up-to-date overview of the current state of global carbon markets, examining key trends, market dynamics, and emerging developments that shape the landscape of emissions trading.

Global Carbon Market Size and Value:

The size and value of the global carbon market continue to expand, reflecting the growing importance of carbon pricing in the transition to a low-carbon economy. As of the latest assessments, the market size has reached [provide approximate value], encompassing diverse market mechanisms, including cap-and-trade systems, carbon taxes, and voluntary markets.

Cap-and-Trade Systems:

Cap-and-trade systems remain prominent contributors to the global carbon market. Established systems such as the European Union Emissions Trading System (EU ETS) and emerging markets like China's national Emission Trading System (ETS) significantly influence the overall market dynamics.

Voluntary Carbon Markets:

Voluntary carbon markets have experienced substantial growth, driven by corporate commitments to sustainability and climate action. Businesses and individuals participate in voluntary markets to offset their carbon footprints, driving demand for high-quality carbon credits and creating a diverse array of emissions reduction projects.

Regional Variances and Initiatives:

The current state of global carbon markets exhibits regional variances, with different jurisdictions implementing diverse approaches to carbon pricing.

Europe:

Europe continues to lead in carbon market development, with the EU ETS undergoing reforms and strengthening its role as a model for cap-and-trade systems. The European Green Deal further solidifies the region's commitment to ambitious emission reduction targets.

Asia:

Asia, home to significant emissions contributors like China, has been actively expanding its carbon market initiatives. The implementation of China's national ETS and other regional efforts underscores the region's increasing role in shaping global carbon markets.

North America:

In North America, various jurisdictions are advancing carbon market agendas. The collaboration between California and Quebec's cap-and-trade systems and the ongoing discussions about carbon pricing mechanisms at the national level in the United States contribute to the region's evolving carbon market landscape.

Emerging Market Mechanisms and Innovations:

Innovations within carbon markets continue to emerge, with a focus on enhancing efficiency, transparency, and environmental integrity.

Article 6 of the Paris Agreement:

The implementation of Article 6 of the Paris Agreement, addressing international cooperation in emissions trading, is gaining momentum. Countries are exploring opportunities for collaboration and the development of new market mechanisms to support their Nationally Determined Contributions (NDCs).

Digital Platforms and Blockchain:

Digital platforms and blockchain technology are increasingly being explored to enhance transparency and streamline transactions in carbon markets. These innovations have the potential to facilitate the efficient tracking and trading of carbon credits, reducing administrative complexities.

Challenges and Opportunities:

The current state of global carbon markets is characterized by both challenges and opportunities that impact market participants and stakeholders.

Challenges:

Challenges include the need for standardized methodologies, addressing concerns about the potential for carbon market manipulation, and ensuring that market mechanisms align with international climate goals. Regulatory uncertainties and variations across jurisdictions also pose challenges for market participants.

Opportunities:

Opportunities abound for market participants to capitalize on the growing demand for emissions reductions. The voluntary carbon market offers businesses and individuals a platform to support sustainability goals, while advancements in technology and international collaborations create opportunities for innovation and market expansion.

The current state of global carbon markets reflects a dynamic and evolving landscape. With a growing market size, regional variations, and ongoing innovations, carbon markets are positioned as crucial instruments in the fight against climate change. As countries and businesses increasingly embrace carbon pricing mechanisms, the global carbon market is poised to play an even more significant role in shaping a sustainable and low-carbon future. Market participants and stakeholders should stay informed about developments, navigate challenges, and leverage opportunities to contribute meaningfully to the global effort to reduce greenhouse gas emissions.

9.2 Predicting Future Trends and Opportunities in The Sector

As the global community intensifies its efforts to combat climate change, the landscape of carbon markets and trading continues to evolve. In this chapter, we explore the emerging trends and potential opportunities that are likely to shape the future of carbon markets.

Technological Advancements:

The carbon markets of the future will undoubtedly be influenced by advancements in technology. The integration of blockchain and artificial intelligence (AI) into carbon trading platforms is expected to enhance transparency, streamline processes, and reduce transaction costs. Smart contracts powered by blockchain could automate the verification and validation of carbon credits, making the entire process more efficient and trustworthy.

Furthermore, satellite technology and remote sensing capabilities are becoming increasingly sophisticated. These technologies can play a pivotal role in monitoring and verifying emissions reductions, providing a more accurate and real-time measurement of carbon sequestration activities. As technology continues to advance, the precision and reliability of carbon market data are likely to improve significantly.

Regulatory Developments:

Governments around the world are recognizing the urgency of addressing climate change and are implementing more ambitious emission reduction targets. This increased commitment is expected to result in stricter regulations and expanded carbon markets. Policymakers may introduce new trading mechanisms, extend existing cap-and-trade systems, or develop regional and international collaborations to create a more comprehensive and interconnected carbon market.

Market participants should closely monitor these regulatory developments to adapt their strategies and seize emerging opportunities. The integration of carbon pricing into broader environmental and economic policies may further enhance the effectiveness of carbon markets as a tool for achieving climate goals.

Growing Demand for Nature-Based Solutions:

Nature-based solutions, such as reforestation, afforestation, and sustainable land management, are gaining traction as effective means of sequestering carbon. The carbon markets of the future are likely to see a surge in demand for nature-based carbon credits as businesses and governments seek to offset their emissions through environmentally friendly projects.

Investors and project developers should explore partnerships that focus on nature-based solutions, recognizing the potential for both environmental impact and financial returns. Additionally, the development of standardized methodologies for measuring and verifying carbon removals from nature-based projects will be crucial to ensure the credibility and integrity of such credits.

Social and Corporate Responsibility:

Increasing awareness of climate change and the need for sustainable business practices is driving companies to adopt more environmentally responsible strategies. As consumers and investors prioritize sustainability, corporations are integrating carbon neutrality goals into their business models. This shift in mindset creates opportunities for companies to engage in carbon markets, either by reducing their own emissions or investing in carbon offset projects.

Carbon trading platforms that facilitate corporate engagement in carbon markets may see a surge in demand. Companies that proactively participate in these markets not only contribute to climate action but also enhance their reputation and stakeholder relationships.

Global Collaboration and Carbon Pricing Mechanisms:

The success of carbon markets depends on international cooperation and the establishment of common standards. Global collaborations, such as the Paris Agreement, aim to create a unified approach to addressing climate change. Future carbon markets may witness increased harmonization of carbon pricing mechanisms, creating a more interconnected and efficient global market.

Market participants should be prepared to navigate evolving international frameworks and explore opportunities arising from cross-border collaboration. As countries work together to achieve common climate goals, the potential for linking regional carbon markets and creating a truly global carbon market becomes increasingly plausible.

In conclusion, the future of carbon markets and trading holds promise and challenges in equal measure. Technological innovations, regulatory developments, the rise of nature-based solutions, corporate responsibility, and global collaboration are key factors shaping the landscape. Staying informed, adaptable, and proactive will be essential for businesses, investors, and policymakers seeking to capitalize on the evolving opportunities in the dynamic world of carbon markets.

9.3 Forecasting the Potential Impact of Emerging Technologies on Carbon Markets

The intersection of technology and environmental sustainability has the potential to revolutionize carbon markets. In this chapter, we delve into the emerging technologies that are poised to shape the future of carbon markets and explore the forecasted impact on trading, transparency, and overall market dynamics.

Blockchain and Smart Contracts:

Blockchain technology, with its decentralized and tamper-resistant ledger system, has gained attention for its potential to enhance transparency and traceability in carbon markets. Smart contracts, self-executing contracts with coded terms, have the capability to automate various aspects of carbon trading, including verification, issuance, and retirement of carbon credits.

Forecasters anticipate that blockchain and smart contracts will significantly reduce the risk of fraud and improve the efficiency of transactions. As these technologies mature, carbon markets may experience streamlined processes, reduced transaction costs, and increased trust among market participants.

Artificial Intelligence and Data Analytics:

The utilization of artificial intelligence (AI) and advanced data analytics holds great promise for enhancing the accuracy of emissions measurements and the validation of carbon offset projects. AI algorithms can process vast amounts of data from diverse sources, such as satellite imagery and IoT devices, to provide real-time insights into emissions and sequestration activities.

The forecasted impact of AI in carbon markets includes improved monitoring, reporting, and verification processes. AI-powered tools can help identify potential anomalies, assess project performance, and contribute to a more reliable and transparent carbon market ecosystem.

Tokenization of Carbon Credits:

Tokenization involves representing real-world assets, such as carbon credits, as digital tokens on a blockchain. This emerging technology has the potential to increase liquidity in carbon markets by fractionalizing carbon credits and enabling broader participation from a diverse range of investors.

Forecasters suggest that tokenization could democratize access to carbon markets, allowing smaller investors to contribute to climate mitigation efforts. The increased liquidity may also foster secondary markets for carbon credits, providing new opportunities for trading and investment.

Quantum Computing:

While still in its early stages, quantum computing holds the potential to revolutionize complex calculations involved in carbon market modeling, scenario analysis, and risk assessment. Quantum computers can process vast datasets and perform computations at speeds unimaginable with classical computers.

The forecasted impact of quantum computing on carbon markets includes faster and more accurate carbon pricing models, improved risk management strategies, and enhanced scenario planning. As quantum computing technology matures, it may offer a competitive advantage to those who can harness its power in the carbon trading space.

Internet of Things (IoT) and Remote Sensing:

The proliferation of IoT devices and advancements in remote sensing technologies provide unprecedented opportunities for real-time monitoring and verification of emissions reductions and carbon sequestration activities. IoT devices deployed in various industries can continuously collect and transmit data, contributing to a more robust and accurate measurement of carbon-related activities.

Forecasters anticipate that integrating IoT and remote sensing technologies will enhance the credibility of carbon credits by providing continuous and verifiable data. This may lead to increased investor confidence and a more dynamic and responsive carbon market.

In conclusion, the forecasted impact of emerging technologies on carbon markets is multifaceted, offering opportunities for increased efficiency, transparency, and innovation. Market participants, policymakers, and investors should closely monitor these technological advancements and adapt their strategies to leverage the potential benefits of these transformative tools in the evolving landscape of carbon markets.

Way Forward

As we conclude this comprehensive guide to carbon markets and trading, it's evident that we stand at the intersection of environmental stewardship, economic innovation, and technological evolution. The journey through the preceding chapters has explored the intricacies of carbon markets, delving into the mechanisms, challenges, and opportunities that define this critical facet of the global response to climate change.

Reflecting on the Present

The present state of carbon markets is marked by a growing recognition of the urgent need for collective action to address climate change. Countries, corporations, and individuals are increasingly acknowledging the role of carbon markets as instrumental tools for achieving emissions reduction targets and promoting sustainable practices. The establishment of cap-and-trade systems, carbon offset projects, and international agreements such as the Paris Agreement reflects the global commitment to fostering a low-carbon future.

Acknowledging Challenges

Despite the progress made, challenges persist. Carbon markets face issues of integrity, transparency, and the need for more ambitious emission reduction targets. The evolution of standards, methodologies, and regulatory frameworks is an ongoing process requiring adaptability and collaboration. Overcoming these challenges necessitates a collective effort from governments, businesses, and civil society to create a robust and effective global carbon market.

Embracing Innovation

Innovation stands as a beacon of hope in the journey towards a sustainable future. Emerging technologies, such as blockchain, artificial intelligence, and the Internet of Things, offer unprecedented opportunities to enhance the efficiency, transparency, and inclusivity of carbon markets.

As we look to the future, the integration of these technologies may reshape the landscape, creating a more dynamic, responsive, and interconnected global carbon market.

Seizing Opportunities

The forecasted trends and opportunities outlined in the preceding chapters underscore the potential for growth and impact within the carbon market space. Nature-based solutions, corporate responsibility, global collaboration, and the tokenization of carbon credits are among the avenues that hold promise for market participants seeking to align environmental goals with economic interests.

The Imperative of Action

In the face of the existential threat posed by climate change, the imperative of action is clear. This guide aims to equip stakeholders–ranging from policymakers and businesses to investors and individuals–with the knowledge to navigate the complexities of carbon markets. The decisions made in the coming years will shape the trajectory of our planet's environmental health and the well-being of future generations.

A Call for Collaboration

As we move forward, collaboration emerges as the linchpin for success. Governments, businesses, and communities must collaborate on a global scale, sharing insights, best practices, and innovations. The inclusive participation of diverse stakeholders is essential to create a carbon market ecosystem that is resilient, equitable, and capable of driving meaningful climate action.

A Resilient Future

In closing, the journey through this guide invites all participants in the carbon market arena to embrace a mindset of resilience, adaptability, and responsibility.

The challenges may be formidable, but so too are the opportunities for positive change. By working together and leveraging the tools at our disposal, we can shape a future where carbon markets play a pivotal role in fostering a sustainable and resilient world.

This guide is not the end but rather a waypoint in the ongoing narrative of our shared commitment to addressing climate change. The path forward may be challenging, but with dedication, innovation, and collective action, we can navigate the evolving terrain of carbon markets towards a future that is both economically prosperous and environmentally sustainable.

Dr. Chirag Bhimani

Notes

www.ingramcontent.com/pod-product-compliance
Lightning Source LLC
LaVergne TN
LVHW061548070526
838199LV00077B/6954